String Qu

Ludwig van Beethoven

Op. 135

Performer's Edition

C-00017-PS

© 2009 Performer's Edition
Indianapolis, Indiana

All rights reserved.
No part of this publication may be reproduced,
stored electronically, or transmitted in any form
without the written consent of the publisher.

String Quartet No. 16
Op. 135
Ludwig van Beethoven

String Quartet No. 16

String Quartet No. 16

String Quartet No. 16

String Quartet No. 16

String Quartet No. 16

String Quartet No. 16

String Quartet No. 16

String Quartet No. 16

String Quartet No. 16

String Quartet No. 16

String Quartet No. 16

2.

String Quartet No. 16

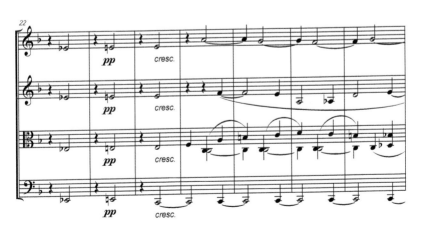

String Quartet No. 16

String Quartet No. 16

String Quartet No. 16

String Quartet No. 16

String Quartet No. 16

String Quartet No. 16

String Quartet No. 16

String Quartet No. 16

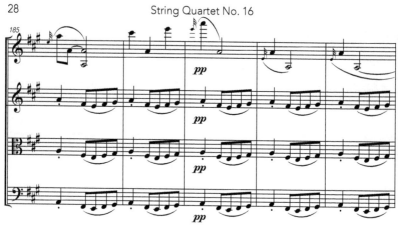

String Quartet No. 16

String Quartet No. 16

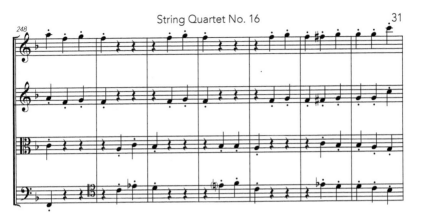

String Quartet No. 16

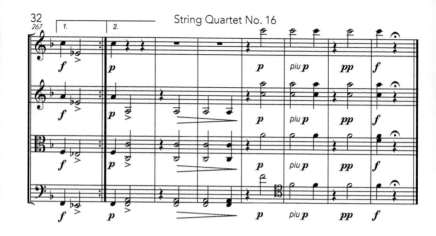

3.

Lento assai, cantante e tranquillo

String Quartet No. 16

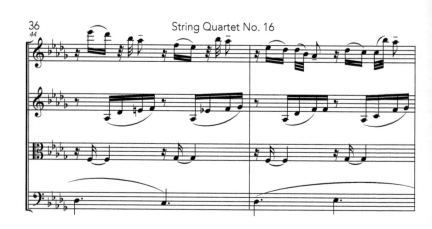

String Quartet No. 16

String Quartet No. 16

String Quartet No. 16

String Quartet No. 16

String Quartet No. 16

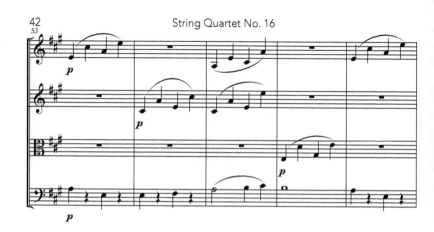

String Quartet No. 16

String Quartet No. 16

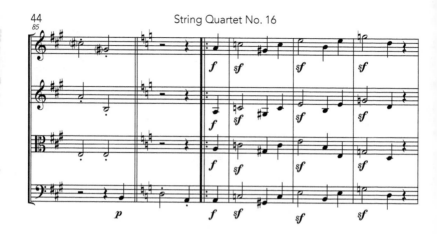

String Quartet No. 16

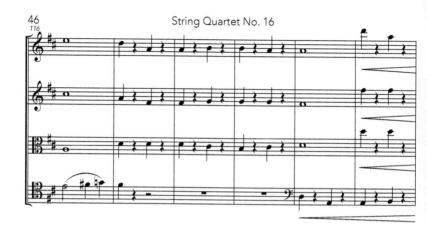

String Quartet No. 16

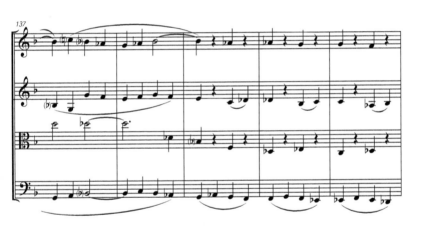

String Quartet No. 16

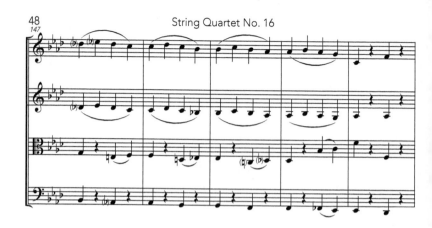

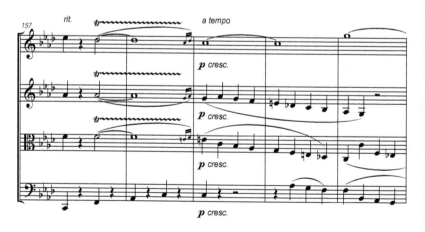

String Quartet No. 16

Grave ma non troppo tratto

String Quartet No. 16

String Quartet No. 16

String Quartet No. 16

String Quartet No. 16

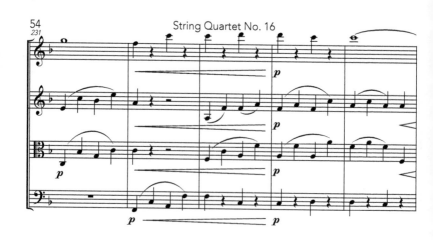

String Quartet No. 16 Poco adagio

String Quartet No. 16